YOU GOT THE JOB

YOU GOT THE JOB

Be Job Ready Get Hired

Authored by

PRADDEEP KHAANAPURE

WINGS PUBLICATION INTERNATIONAL

WE GIVE WINGS TO YOUR DREAM!

Disclaimer

This book has been published with all reasonable efforts taken to make the material error-free after the consent of the author. This book is sold subject to the condition that it shall not, by way of trade or otherwise, be lent, resold, or otherwise circulated without the copyright owner's prior written consent in any form of binding or cover other than that in which it is published and without a similar condition including this condition being imposed on the subsequent purchaser and without limiting the rights under copyright reserved above, no part of this publication maybe reproduced, stored in or introduced into a retrieval system or transmitted in any form or by any other means without the permission of the copyright owner.

WINGS PUBLICATION INTERNATIONAL
WE GIVE WINGS TO YOUR DREAM!

Registered Office- Wings Publication International
Sharjah Publishing City, Sharjah, United Arab Emirate (UAE)
Website: http://www. wingspublication. com
Email: mybook@wingspublication. com

First Published by **WINGS PUBLICATION INTERNATIONAL 2019**

Title: **You Got the Job**

Price: ₹599 | $12

ISBN 978-93-89024-59-3

LIMITS OF LIABILITY/DISCLAIMER OF WARRANTY

The Author of this book is solely responsible and liable for its content including but not limited to the views, representations, descriptions, statements, information, opinions and references. The information presented in this book is solely compiled by the Author from sources believed to be accurate and the Publisher assumes no responsibility for any errors or omissions. The information is not intended to replace or substitute professional advice.

The Content of this book shall not constitute or be construed or deemed to reflect the opinion or expression of the Publisher. Publisher of this book does not endorse or approve any content of this book or guarantee the reliability, accuracy or completeness of the content published herein and do not make any representations or warranties of any kind, express or implied, including but not limited to the implied warranties of merchantability, fitness for a particular purpose. The Publisher shall not be held liable whatsoever for any errors, omissions, whether such errors or omissions result from negligence, accident, or any other cause or claims for loss or damages of any kind, including without limitation, indirect or consequential loss or damage arising out of use, inability to use, or about the reliability, accuracy or sufficiency of the information contained in this book. All disputes are subject to Indore (M. P.) jurisdiction only.

Dedicated to...

As I start sharing my knowledge with you today, I thank Lord Ganesh to have blessed me to share these strategies that will help get closer to the job you desire.

I dedicate this book to you as the reader, as you are an inspiration for me to write. You picked up this book today with an intent to be job-ready and that is my biggest inspiration to pen down my thoughts, I exist as an Author & a Coach today because you are seeking guidance. This book is dedicated to all the students whom I have coached and helped to date in the least possible way that I could.

I am thankful to my family and closest friends who stood by me and supported me in their own ways to ensure I publish this book.

I thank all my teachers including life for choosing me to teach amazing lessons, to inspire and motivate me to get back up every time I fall back.

Best Regards
Praddeep Khaanapure

Acknowledgment

I would like to thank Lord Ganesha first, as I personally believe is the real Vignaharta, I seek his blessings as I start to pen down my knowledge that I have received over a period of time.

I thank my wife Rohee & my son Shaurya who have been supportive & patient throughout this process. Their sacrifice on their personal time helped me write the book with clarity & focus.

I am thankful to my amazing, craziest friends who supported me in every possible way to ensure this book reaches you. Naming all of them would not be possible but I am grateful to God to bless me with such amazing people in my life.

Of the many Trainers, I am thankful to the 2 best Trainers and Author who have inspired me a lot, Simon Sinek through "Start with Why" & Stephen Covey through, "7 habits of Highly Effective People". These 2 books changed my thinking a lot & made me who I am today.

I dedicate this book to every job seeker and an employee out there who has a lot of potential & can grow in their life & are just seeking an opportunity to showcase their talent. This book belongs to everyone who wants to believe in themselves.

Best Regards
Praddeep Khaanapure

Preface

Let me tell you a story about a boy called Akash.

Akash like everyone else was graduating from college and was clueless on what to do after graduation. Some people suggested him to do further studies and said only PG/ MBAs have a value, some people suggested do a specialized certification or course that offers job guarantee.

Some people suggested get in "some" job and then after 2 years do an MBA and then become a manager, life will be set. Parents behaved either they have done with their responsibilities by making him a graduate or they forced him to get a "secured" job.

He went to a cyber cafe and made a resume for himself which the cafe guy charged about 50 Rs to make his resume which he made by simply editing his personal details and gave him the printout which Akash was clueless on what to do. Someone suggested to upload it on portals and also on social sites like LinkedIn.

He did the same and the first thing that happened was he got a call from few consultants for a sales job or he got calls from fraudulent consultancy who tried taking money from him claiming that he is selected for a big corporate job and this is the security amount that he needs to pay to secure his job.

Frustrated and angered Akash started believing that there are no jobs in the market and possibly left with only one option, beg for a job from anyone and everyone he could connect with.

This is the dilemma of most of the graduating freshers today. There are many who will suggest and give others advice but rarely who will guide. What people don't realize while advising is that they are probably misleading someone unknowingly.

PG students are in a bigger dilemma, they spend lakhs of rupees and yet are either still looking for a job or working against their dream jobs that they thought they would get before enrolling. Most of the job seekers are frustrated today and follow the herd mentality.

In the most advanced technology era also people still go about asking anyone and everyone….. "koi job opening hai to bata naa" meaning let me know if any job opportunities for me.

There are platforms like job portals and LinkedIn that are made only for job seekers but because no one is there to tell us how the jo portals work or how sites like

LinkedIn are misused rather makes it difficult for anyone to search for a job.

To understand the dilemma of these job seekers, let's look at a few actual facts published between 2018 & 2019.

1. 52.5% respondents feel job scenario in India has worsened: RBI (source article link below)

   https://www.peoplematters.in/news/jobs/525-respondents-feel-job-scenario-in-india-has-worsened-rbi-23357?utm_source=peoplematters&utm_medium=interstitial&utm_campaign=learnings-of-the-day

2. The proportion of formally skilled workers in India is extremely low, at 4.69% of the total workforce, compared to 24% in China, 52% in the US, 68% in the UK, 75% in Germany, 80% in Japan and 96% in South Korea. (source article link below)

   https://www.financialexpress.com/opinion/skill-india-why-there-is-a-gap-between-current-status-and-goals-explained/1520633/

   An interesting point mentioned in the article is quoted as it is below

   The mismatch between skills, academic training and employment has broadened to an extent where, on the one hand, employers are unable to discover suitably trained people, and on the other, the youth is unable to find the kind of jobs they aspire to for. According to the latest India Skill Report (2019), only 45.6% of the youth graduating from educational institutions are employable.

An article published in Forbes India site mentioned the below

3. India is Creating Millions of High Skilled Jobs, But Its Education System Isn't Keeping Up. (source link mentioned below)

   https://www.forbes.com/sites/prakashmallya/2018/05/06/india-is-creating-millions-of-high-skilled-jobs-but-its-education-system-isnt-keeping-up/#69a94f56480f

Quoting few takeaways as mentioned by the author below

- India would need to create 8.1 million jobs annually, against the 5.5 million created in 2017, to keep employment rates constant between 2015 and 2025.
- Public spending on education in India is 3.8% of the GDP, lower than countries such as Brazil and Malaysia
- It is estimated that there will be 104.62 million fresh entrants in the labor market by 2022; in fact, India would need to create 8.1 million jobs annually, against the 5.5 million created in 2017, to keep employment rates constant between 2015 and 2025.

The education system and syllabus haven't kept up with the fast-changing business needs, especially those that are interlinked to soft skills, advanced technology adoption, and even the flexibility to re-skill for emerging opportunities.

The problem job seekers face today is that there are very few knowledgeable coaches and guides who help them to search for a job. As the education industry is non-regulated there are so many institutions that fool people by offering job guarantee programs.

This book is my attempt in breaking the herd mentality and to also provide a clear step by step process to prepare for the interview without enrolling for any high paying courses or PG certification just to get a job.

There are 10 Steps mentioned and if you follow them well you will be 100 % ready to handle any interview and also be able to search for a job without anyone's help.

This book contains simple steps processes/secrets that come from more than 7 years of coaching students and job seekers on the successful job search process and I want to share this knowledge and coaching through which I can benefit as many job seekers as I can.

One of the biggest advantages of this book is it will help you know how the candidate selection process happens and helps you search the job without asking anyone for any job openings. To gain the maximum benefit from this book, please complete all the assignments in every chapter before moving to the next one. This book is meant to make you think and prepare. If you apply the learning, the results are guaranteed to come.

I say this with confidence based on the success stories that happened when job seekers have applied the learning. I have trained and coached over 6,000 students who have benefitted from this program and with their best wishes, I am able to share this with you today so that you can benefit & get the job you are looking for.

Now grab a pencil and highlight areas that you would like to come back and read again. Start applying the learning from every chapter one by one and don't be in a hurry to finish the book. Learn, digest the lesson, make notes and most important: Take actions.

Nothing will be of any use if you don't take action.

Results will come to the one who constantly takes action. Good Luck and let's get started.

How to use this Book?

To make the best out of this guide, Act on every chapter. Success in any area is the outcome of knowledge and action. I have made this genuine attempt to pass all the knowledge that I have gathered over the last 7 years & am penning the knowledge in this guide which was due for a long time.

I being an HR myself & with constant interaction from fellow colleagues across all the Industries, I have made a simple yet very effective step that prepares you for any Interview. Most of the steps are mentioned for the first time. I honestly haven't spent much effort on telling you what to wear and what not to hear. I am already making an assumption that you are well aware of how to go for an Interview.

This book is not free advice on how to please the Interviewer and be extra sweet or nice and be a Yes man to everything just to get the job, but it's written with an intent to help you understand how difficult it is for the HR team to get a candidate on board.

A simple process guide that helps you search the job the right way & help you prepare for the Interview completely.

It is not a onetime read, let alone not a motivational book at all. This book is to make you think and act. You have to act on the knowledge shared.

Every chapter is designed to help you break the herd mentality. The core objective of this book is to make you a professional who is giving an Interview for 2 reasons. The first is to get selected and the second is to decide if you want to say yes to that Job. It may sound funny now but I assure you that you will agree with me by the time you finish this book.

Today with the advancement of Technology, we are changing many habits of our and adapting to the latest trends. We have the latest gadgets, latest fashion, latest lifestyle & definitely very happy people on Social Media sites but for decades now, people still search for jobs the traditional way.

Time has changed; the digital world demands us to be in limelight and in demand. Organizations need talented and skilled people as much as the person needs the job. It is a mutually beneficial world. Organizations are realizing the importance of hiring the right person for the role and especially the ones who can stay long and continue to add value to the organization.

As Simon Sinek says, ask yourself all the time Why do you do what you do? My why is to help the people search for jobs based on the actual job process across the Industry.

This book is useful for any job seeker; there are no specific age criteria that are applicable to read. Anyone can use this book and reap the benefits of the book. So, I wish you all the best to learn the steps that will get you closer to your desired job.

Let's get started

Contents

CHAPTER *One*

The Interview Process: How the Actual Selection Process Works

The idea behind sharing the hiring process is to help you understand the complete truth about hiring. Over the last many years, I have seen many candidates getting nervous and being timid while giving Interviews which in their real-life they are not. These are confident people who have spoken to many strangers very boldly & have ventured in unknown areas without any fear but go completely blank when they face an Interview. I myself have been nervous so many times during the first 5 years of my career.

I used to feel intimidated by the person on the other side and felt I was getting interrogated and legs trembled most of the time.

A lot of freshers including Management & Engineering College students have been a victim of such situations. When I started recruitment, I was surprised to know how tedious the task of HR is to hire one potential candidate for the role. You know some times, it takes more than a month to select the candidate & yet there is no guarantee that the selected candidate will come on board.

Let's look at the hiring process from the candidate's side and also from inside the HR Chamber.

For the candidate, here is how it works. You can add/ delete based on the city you are looking for a job in.

The first step is to make a good resume. Then upload the same on job portals & professional networking site. Then search the jobs online/ offline, share it with our network.

Going through the aptitude tests in some cases, then the GD, Personal Interview round with HR, Functional/ Technical Manager depending on the role you are seeking and then again discussion with HR for Salary & joining.

Sounds simple, isn't it? We will discuss our steps in detail over the entire book especially mistakes we do and correct them to get fine-tune results.

Now let's look at the other side of the table & see what goes into the HR department.

Step 1: The Recruitment team gets the candidate recruitment from the particular department then the JD (job description) is created based on the skill sets required for the role. Upon the JD approval, the same is posted on job portals, professional networking sites like LinkedIn/ shared with job consultants and also in fewer companies shared within the company with the existing employees as well.

Step 2: Go to portals and search for the candidate's profile (this is really tedious as they have to shortlist only relevant profiles amongst the thousands of profiles & most of them are not relevant for the role but showed up because one or two skill sets match. Shortlist the candidates, share the same with business heads/ managers.

Let's say they get about 1000 relevant profiles; the Recruiter will download the first 50 max in the first go and then share the same with business and about 20 will be shortlisted for the telephonic/ video/ personal round.

Step 3: Calling the potential candidates for the Interview & then conduct the rounds which most of you are aware as you are involved in the process. Here is the interesting part. If there were 15 candidates lined up for the Interview, about 50% drop out most of the time, common dropouts are the one who are already working. (We will see later why the drop out)

With the 50% who turned up, discuss, negotiate, convince the selected one to join at the package negotiated & hope all goes well until the person comes on board. There is also a fear that during the joining time, the candidate might join somewhere or may get retained by his organization.

Now imagine the dilemma of the HR personnel whose daily job is to call candidates for Interviews, does it sound like these are the same HR Managers who meet us with so much confidence? The pressure of hiring is tremendous on them as well.

Recruitment requires a lot of patience & if you recall your Interview, you might remember the HR was calm and composed, professional and was convincing you about the role and the company as much as they were interviewing you.

Recruitment is a 2-way process, HR's are trained well to conduct Interviews in the most professional way, there are proper coaching and guidance at every level. Even HR personnel get nervous while conducting Interviews but that will never reflect in their day to day Interviewing process.

This is how the recruitment process works and the objective of every HR is to get the right candidate at the right price.

The idea behind sharing this with you to help you understand that the stress and pressure you are under is also the same for the HR. Just like you are seeking an opportunity, there is someone looking for the skill sets you possess. Once you understand the process, it becomes easier for you to search the jobs & crack the Interviews based on the preparation you have done.

If you observe, the only place HR search for candidates is either on Job Portals or on sites like LinkedIn. Hence you need to understand how the portals and LinkedIn work.

One of the best bargains of this book is you will learn how the portals work & once you understand you join the 5% category of people who knows how to use the portals to ensure you land up with the right Interview call.

Maybe going forward, it will be advisable to stop asking anyone and everyone for a job, because that's not how jobs are shared.

Let's focus on the first 2 chapters, the Resume building and how to use job portals, these chapters are little technical hence requesting you to pay a little more attention here and do the tasks step by step.

CHAPTER *Two*

Winning Strategies for a Professional Resume

I have an exercise for you. Take a pen and paper. Evaluate the below CV & answer 2 questions: Will you shortlist this CV for a job? If Yes then How much Salary will you offer and what post will you offer?

Ready? Here We Go

Johny White

MOBILE: 000000000000

E-MAIL: jhonnywh@hotmail.com

Objective:

To achieve a position in a challenging environment that will allow me to contribute to the success of an organization by utilizing my skills and walking the extra mile.

Educational Qualifications:

Post Graduation Diploma in Business Management

[XYZ of Learning, Argentina] **[2008]**

Bachelors in Commerce [B.Com] (Computer Applications)

[South Chennai University, India] **[2003]**

Achievement

I was nominated, best employee of the year 2007 by the XYZ ABC Government.

Work Experience:

Marigold Bpo Ltd. [Oct 2012 – till date] in XYZ Express Customer Services Uk.

1. Booking collections for UK customers
2. Provide quote to the customers
3. Logistics tracking
4. Handling queries

XYZ Exports India. [Nov 2010 –Oct 2012] ***Business Development***

XYZ Association Recreation Centre, Mumbai [Aug 2009 – Nov 2010] ***Executive Business Development***

One of the most exclusive and high profile recreation centre's in the heart of BKC.

XYZ PLC, ABC PVT London [OCT 2007-DEC 2008] ***Executive Services Food & Beverage***

One of best Ale beer makers in UK and owns more than 300 pubs in London.

XYZ group of Hotels, XXXXX, British Isles, UK [DEC 2006-SEP 2007]

Supervisor One of best 3 star chain of hotels on the XXXXX

XXXXX Pvt. Ltd, Mumbai, India [AUG 2005-SEP 2006] ***Management Trainee***

XXXXXX Services Private Ltd, Mumbai, India [APR 2004-MAY 2005] ***Human Resources & Admin***

XXXX & XXX. Chartered Accountant's Firm [MAY 2002-JUNE 2003] ***Audit Assistant***

SKILLS:

Office applications: Microsoft office suite (**Word, Excel, PowerPoint, Outlook, Access**)

REFERENCE: AVAILABLE ON REQUEST

What do you think of the above profile? Make your view and write your observation on the same.

Let's look at one more.

RESUME

Jack Brown

Address: 'XXXX', Hs no. XXX, AAAAA, AAAA, XXXX(w) Dist-Thane

Phone No: 9797979797

Email: jackbrown@ymail.com

Career Objective:

"I want to service an organization with integrity and get a depth knowledge of the Organization I work in"

Education qualification:

Degree	University	School/ College	Percentage
SSC	Mah.State board	XXXXX School	62%
HSC	Mah.State board	XXXXX Junior College	64%
Bach. banking & Insurance	Mumbai University	XXXXX Degree College	63%

Other Couses: Completed MS-CIT(computer basic knowledge) with 76%

Academic Project:

Project Title: 'CRM IN NEW GENERATION BANKS: A CASE STUDY OF XXXX BANK'

Achievement:

- Have done social service of 100 hours with XXXX
- Academic Achievement:
    1. Participated in in Junior college 'Short Put' (2nd place) and 'Discuss Throw'(3rd place)
    2. Represented Junior College in 'Short Put'(3rd place) and 'Discuss Throw'(3rd place).
    3. Represented Junior College Football Team at District and Taluka level.

Strength:

- Good communication skills
- A depth Learner
- Team player

Hobbies and Intersects

Working out in gym, playing soccer, reading, listening to soft music.

Personal Detail:

D.O.B: 1st January XXXX

Passport Details: X11111 **Validity:** 11/02/2222

Languages Known: English, Hindi, Marathi, Gujrathi

Marital Status: Single

I hereby declare that all the information provide by me in this application is factual and correct to best of my knowledge and belief.

What is your analysis of the same?

Did you hire anyone? If yes how much salary? I am sure by now you must have got an image of the person in front of you based on the profile you saw. Have you ever hired anyone or ever done a course on shortlisting resumes, No right? Yet you were able to analyze the results and make a selection on what to do with the resumes. You got the idea of how the impression is built through the resume.

Throughout our academics, we were never made realize the importance of a professional resume and hence we never paid attention to either. Thousands of talented and skilled people are yet to receive an Interview call because of one primary reason, Resume not made professionally.

Secret 1: Your Resume decides the selection to the maximum extent. As mentioned earlier, out of about 1000 people who are eligible for the role only about 50 people get an opportunity to give the interview and primarily the way the resume is made decides if you will get the Interview call or not.

HR look for skill sets that match the role, apart from that the clarity in which you have written sentences & key highlighters makes a lot of difference. The resume is our first impression that opens the door to a new opportunity even before we meet the HR. It describes our personality, our professionalism and also most of the time, our pay capability.

Let's get going and build a professional resume for yourself: The following steps are involved in building a resume that I have included for the fresher as well experienced on. You can use the sections as per your need & experience

1. Personal Details
2. Summary/ Career objective
3. Education Details
4. Projects

5. Work Experience
6. Co-curricular Activities

Section 1: Personal Details

Just the basic information is sufficient in the personal details,

1. Your full name, mailing address with pin code (Even the location with pin code is acceptable). There are many organizations that would want to know the commute time you will take or they may have picked up drop services and have geographical boundaries hence they would want to know the Pin code.
2. Email id should be simple as it can be, numbers in email id should be relevant.
   a. Eg: avkaashkumar@gmail.com, ankit.verma1904@gmail.com
3. Avoid funny email address like handsomeanil143@ rocketmail.com
4. Mention one active mobile number, landline should be home number only
5. Languages are known should be mentioned only if special cases Like French, German, Sanskrit, etc.
6. Date of birth and Age is optional information.

   Things irrelevant to the job profile and need to be avoided are

7. Religion, Nationality, Marital Status, Family details, Passport, References, etc.

Personal details should be concise and in brief.

Here is how the personal details should look like

First Name Last Name
Contact No.: +910000000000 **E-Mail**: xxxxxxx
XXXXXXXXXXXXXXXX Pune-412307
Date of Birth: xx/xx/xxxx

Education

I personally believe we have kept the education as the only thing that is important in our profile that is probably the reason, we are so obsessed about putting the education details on the box. Jokes apart, Even I am not sure why we put the education in the box all the time.

But it is actually not a good idea to put the education in the box, it simply spoils the structure of the resume.

There is no need for a separate box and the education details should be written in sentences. Mention any ongoing education you are pursuing including certifications or short courses including along with the graduation and post-graduation.

List a minimum of two and max four education details in the resume.

Mention certifications or courses only if they are relevant to the opening. So, if you are applying for a role in operations no point mentioning you have done certification in digital marketing.

In the Interview, this will lead to many questions around the certification itself and divert the discussion from an operations role to a digital marketing job. But chances are even in the shortlisting process, you will come across as unsure and unclear about your career goals.

Keep the format of the education constant for all certifications and degrees. It includes

1. The program names
2. The Institute name & passing year.
3. Percentage or grade received
4. University Name & City/State, Country.

Mention the same in descending order where you start from the latest one and moving backward year by year.

Optionally you can add your skills and knowledge acquired through important courses and research.

This is how the education details will look like

Workshops & Certifications:

- Pursuing XXXX course- Pune, India.
- XXX XXX XXX XX Certification- Pune, India.
- XXX XXX XXX XXXX Program – Mumbai. India

Scholastics:

- P.G. Diploma in Project management – XXXXXX Institute of Management Studies – Pune.
- XXX XXXX Degree from XXXXX College – Mumbai.

Work Experience

The work experience section is the second most important part of your profile. Don't go up to search the first one thinking you might have missed it, the most important are discussed in a later section of the resume. The Work experience section is an opportunity for you to elaborate on your role and mention your core competencies.

Many people make this mistake of simply writing a few things on their profile and think they will discuss the important ones when they go for the interview. But the problem is you won't get the interview call if HR is not convinced that you are the right person for the role.

That impression comes when you talk about your major roles and responsibilities and achievements in the workplace. Everyone wants to hire a skilled and capable person who can stay long term with them.

Here is how you write this section.

Mention only the last 2 organizations in detail. Other companies can be mentioned below that you worked with at the end of the 2nd organization.

1. Mention the organization tenure in mm yy format.
2. Your designation
3. Your major roles
4. Your achievements

Roles should be a maximum of 6 major ones. Be clear and concise about the roles. The roles should be majorly functional/ technical. The achievements can be as many as you got at the workplace. While talking about achievements, do mention why you got the award. It helps the interviewer know the qualities that you possess without you mentioning separately. Also, include all appreciation and awards received at the workplace. Highlight major changes that you brought in the process if you are working at the Senior position.

Your Work Experience section will look like this

May 2008 – Till date: XXX XXXXX XXXXX Pvt Ltd. India

Designation: Team Manager

Process Handled:Process 1, Process 2, Process 3 and Process 4

Current Process: XXXXX XXXXX XXXX

Journey: Joined as a Process Executive in XXXXX XXXXXX & moved up the ladder to become Team Manager in XXX XXX XXXX Team

- Handling one of the most profitable Process for the Organization where major roles include:
- Working with the Clients and Onshore counterparts for their specific requirements in terms of delivery of functional solutions, specific reporting requirements, process improvements and enhancements (primarily in line with legal and compliance requirements) etc.
- Handling various teams of XXXX XXX viz: BIS Research, Transaction approval, Account opening, Transaction Processing, Account Maintenance, Reconciliation, Cash Management and investigation for High Networth Clients.
- Managing XXX XXXX process (Daily and monthly accounting of XXX XXXX) covering reconciliation of Fund Trades, Cash, Position and

Capital activities between Overseas client, broker and custody, Computation of GAV, NAV and ROR.

- Preparing portfolio valuation report and calculating management fees of investors as per fund prospectus.

Achievements & Recognitions:

- Successful Transition of new work from XXXX location to XXXX location.
- Played a key role in making critical business decisions. Assisted business solution group during feasibility study of new businesses migrating to my team - Recommending KPI, participating in governance calls, overseeing transition till process is BAU, preparing capacity model and agreeing on required resources, preparing Statement of Work and obtaining sign-off with business heads and frequent review thereon.
- Prepared the Transition Feasibility framework for Client services teams.
- Worked on many projects on cost reduction & process efficiency:
    - Automation of Non USD (FX) payments & USD Payments

- Automation of Memo Posting for Incoming funds & Internal Payments
- Automation of Imaging activity to repository
- Project on modification and enhancing System changes in Mint to avoid payment failure in generating MT103

- Completed automation of FX payments project resulting in reduction of 1.5 FTE's and increasing team ability to handle 300% additional volume without increasing FTE.

Academic Projects:

If you are a fresher, include the academic projects along with your education details.

Points to remember are

1. Mention the project name.
2. Description of the project on what was the final outcome
3. A little description of your role in the project.
4. Highlight one of the challenges you faced as a team and what steps you guys took to achieve the target.
   Or
   1. Highlight how you all planned and worked towards achieving the end result.

The Summary & Career objective:

This section is the most important part. This section decides your selection for the Interview. HR's spend an average of 7 to 10 seconds on every resume, the first impression is built in those 10 seconds and the one section where the HR look is by default the summary or the career objective section. Most of the resume has a career objective that is copied from someone else's resume who himself or herself had an idea whom they copied it from.

One example of a terrible Summary line is, "Highly motivated self-driven professional seeking a challenging opportunity with an organization of high repute."

Does it make any sense to you? Does it say anything about the person in brief except for the fact that he/ she is just an air bubble blabbering without any substance inside?

An example of a wrong Career objective is, "Secure a responsible career opportunity to fully utilize my training and skills while making a significant contribution to the success of the company."

Every HR knows this is taken from one of the career sites & hence holds no significant value towards you in spite of this been a perfect objective statement. Let's learn how to write the Summary section first

It has to be simple 2 to 3 sentences/ paragraphs with emphasis on the skillsets you possess and opportunity seeking. For eg:

Fresher's summary statement: Commerce graduate with 1 years' experience in KYC Team, with a flair for learning and self-motivated individual with participation in various debates and presentations, are looking for Opportunities in Investment Banking Operations across any location.

Experienced Summary Statement:

Eg: 1

Dual Master's with specialization in M.Com - Business Administration & MBA – HR with around 2 years' experience in one of the leading Investment Bank in Finance Back Office Operations.

Eg: 2

Passionate in People Interaction & a clear objective to assist people to perform better at work, chose HR as a career option to enable processes in the organization.

Eg: 3

MBA Finance with over a decade with one of the largest Investment Banking was moved from dependence to Independent & now to the Interdependence stage. Currently handling the entire gamut of Private Wealth Management Operations for HNI clients for our International location.

A Summary statement if clearly stated works as a career objective as well, hence there is no need for a career objective. For Professional with more than 3 to 4 companies/ beyond 7 years experience, you should include a professional synopsis about yourself below the summary statement.

A Professional synopsis looks like below

Professional Synopsis

- Results-oriented professional, backed with cross culture behaviour patterns & an excellent career track record in Investment Banking Operations with specialization in Process Migrations, handling start to end of Private Wealth Management for HNI client, Proficient at providing effective leadership results to internal & external clients through effective Process Management, Client Servicing, Timely deliveries & People Management
- Areas of Expertise: Private Wealth Management, Fund Accounting, Reconciliation, Process Migrations, Process Automation Systems, People Management
- Proficientinrunningsuccessfulprocessoperations & experience of developing procedures, service standards for business excellence. Resourceful at maintaining **relationship with internal & cross border clients** to achieve quality product and service norms by resolving their Finance related critical issues

- Fostering a healthy working environment with empathy towards every employee of the organization, handling work schedules, designing KRA's, Selection based on merits for the role, ensuring training and coaching provided on regular basis and regular skip level meets to ensure employees are well taken care of and lead to a better productive team environment. Regular Updates to Senior Management on the overall progress of the Process as well as the Team Members.

For Experienced Professionals, the first page should be primarily Professional Synopsis and Core Competencies that you bring to the table. Eg

Core Competencies

Process Management

- **Team Leadership:** Create, manage, and lead the team, providing appropriate coaching and mentoring along the way for Process Improvisation. Tracking individual contributors and their accomplishments
- **Coaching Skills**: Ability to keep my employees motivated, resolve conflicts and make hard decisions for betterment of process & employees

- **Time Management:** Working with employees, customers and management, often spinning multiple plates at once
- **Budgeting**: Able to keep and maintain a budget in almost every field of the Department
- **Analytical Skills**: Possesses good analytical skills to be able to solve problems that may come up during a typical work day. Able to analyse data and make decisions that affect the project on a regular basis

Learning & Development

- Identifying training needs across levels through mapping of skills required for particular positions and analysis of the existing level of competencies
- Capability Building Initiatives based on organizational Vision & Core values which helped in creating a process driven work environment - Actively Engage, Energize, Lead, Coach, Develop and Retain the Operations Team
- Timely Learning for self as well to work on my own weakness and enhance my core competencies

Performance Management System

- Identify trendsetter ideas by researching industry and implementing tools for better Process Performance

- Enhancement of functional capabilities through Coaching, Mentoring, Job Rotation, and Job Enlargement by reinforcing their positive work contributions and encouraged behaviours that contributed to teamwork
- Defining Roles & Responsibilities, Role Clarity, KRA Driven Performance Management System based on concurrent goals of the organization and measuring performance through a scientific, transparent and participative work culture

Employee Engagement & CSR Initiatives

- One of the core member of BAGWAT Fun Committee, Event Committee, CSR Committee and have conducted various events for employee engagement. Core Objective is to create a happy place to work for & contribute to the Socio-Economic welfare of the underprivileged part of the society
- Regularly conducting events with government schools to educate marginally background students and schools in learning
- Executed many Employee Engagement Programs namely Best Employee of the month, Best Kaizen, Best 5-S Award, Best Quality Award, On the Spot Award, Best Initiative Award, Best Innovation & Creativity Award, Employee of The Year Award, festival celebrations at office for cheering the overall team

This is how the most important section is built. Now task for you before we move ahead,

If you are a Fresher, make 2 summary statements for yourself & If experienced then create 3 Summary statements & highlight core competencies area for yourself.

You can join my mailing list and receive a copy of the sample resume when you share your email address.

CHAPTER *Three*

Secrets About Job Portals: Simple Steps Towards a Successful Interview Call

Secret 2: How the Online search really happens?

For decades, we have not upgraded the way we search for jobs. In my coaching experience over the last 7 years plus, I have come across many people who still share their resume with anyone & literally anyone & expect that they will help them find a job similar to the guy standing outside railway stations in Mumbai sharing the **work from home** template to anyone expecting they will also fall in the trap of making fast money.

We have seen how the HR searches the candidates and this section is all about getting found. The best way to find the job and to get found by HR is Job portals and Social Media.

But because people are unaware of how the job search works, here are a few things that happen through the portals & networking sites most of the time

1. There are various fraudulent consultants who target freshers & first-time job seekers by telling them they are shortlisted & pay a security fee which will be refunded post-training & then disappear after taking the money. Every year, almost 50% of freshers fall into this trap by fraudsters.
2. Social media sites like Linkedin which is one of the best inventions is used as a platform to date. The moment a girl posts that she is seeking jobs or

assistance, loverboys from all age groups are willing to help her but never actually help. They use that opportunity to build a relationship with the person seeking a job. It might sound aggravating but it's the truth. There are many such instances posted every day on LinkedIn.

3. Amazing platforms like Naukri, Times jobs, Shine are under-utilized because job seekers are unaware of how to use them. The reality is platforms like LinkedIn & job portals are a brilliant medium to connect the job seekers & recruiters to come on a single platform.

Let's get going & in this section, we will understand how to use the job portals & social media to get the job you are looking for. Let's start with the job portals.

Job portals sites like Naukri, Times Jobs, Shine and other sites like LinkedIn, incur a heavy cost to offer their service to job seekers, so any ideas on how to make money?

Yes, they charge fees to Corporates & Consultants to give them access to your profile. They offer viewing your profiles & yes it a costly service. Hence Corporates use this service very efficient and are trained on how to use the portals to ensure they get the candidates they are looking for.

Let's understand how a candidate is shortlisted once the Company decides on selecting someone for a particular job role. It's divided in two phases, Shortlisting the profiles & then the Interview. Shortlisting the candidate is completely controlled & done by HR. Business heads will share the skill sets required in the candidate & the HR starts searching the candidate.

Do you think HR's will go about asking people in their network for a candidate with those specific skill sets, the ratio of even getting employee reference is 1 out of 100 people? The only 2 places HR's find the candidates are Job Portals & Social Media Sites. So how do they search a candidate so fast within so many profiles posted on these sites? Here is the secret. The 3 Rules.

The 3 Rules that portals offer to HR

HR's login for candidate search & they will enter the keyword and then apply the three check buttons to search for the candidates. The Keywords are very specific for the role. Only Technical/ Functional skills are mentioned.

For eg. Private Banker, Financial Analyst, Fundamental Research, JAVA, Software developer, Testing, etc. Generic words like good Communication skills, team player, good listeners are not used or else they will never get the desired candidates.

Then they follow the below process for finding the most relevant & desired candidates.

1. Check button no1: Show active candidates over the last 7/15/30/45/60/90/120/6 months/ 1 year: Mostly HR choose the last 7/15/30 days options

2. Check button no 2: show candidates who updated CV in the last 7/15/30/45/60 days: Mostly the choice is between 7 – 45 days
3. Check button no 3: Show most active first.

Post this process, HR's get most of the profiles closest to the one that they are looking for. Now they move to the next step i.e. Resume Headline.

Resume Headline: This is again an important area that will help the HR understand your profile, as this is a paid service for the HR and they have to pay for every profile they check, they read the resume headline and only if it suits the requirement then they will click on your profile.

The resume headline is the summary statement. A clear & crisp statement helps the HR understand the profile in brief. If they click the profile, it means the candidate is a potential one to be called for Interview.

Note to the job seeker: Your resume headline is a make or breaks for your job selection if you are not getting Interview calls, I suggest to make changes in your resume headline. If HR has clicked on the Resume headline, chances are very high that they will call you for the interview discussion.

So, this is how the shortlisting happens. So, here are the steps for you to ensure you get shortlisted by maximum companies

- Fill the complete details in every section, specially Skillsets & Resume Headline.

- Under skill sets, mention functional/ technical skill sets as many as you can but be honest. Don't mention something on which you have no knowledge on.
- Resume Headline has to be specific, brief & should give a brief introduction about yourself.
- Be active as much as you can on the portals through the web. Using portals through the web gives faster results as compared to the app.
- If you are updating your profile on multiple portals, use one portal at one time, don't multitask between portals. For e.g.: Use Naukri for about 30 mins, log out and then log in to Times Jobs, repeat the same for Shine & so one. Recommended is stay active for at least 3 times a day to ensure that your profile is amongst the top page whenever HR's search for candidates.

Now let's learn how to search for jobs on portals.

Jobs Search: Industry & Role

How to make sure you get the right job search

On the main page of the portals, you will see the job section. Once you click on the job search Page, you get various options like search jobs by category, Industry, companies etc.

You need to search for a job by skills, add the skill sets according to your need and search for jobs, and apply for the same. Also mentioned are the contact details of the HR, you can keep it for your reference for follow up on the application.

In some cases, you won't be able to see the contact details, this is where you can take the company's contact details through Google. It is ok to call the HR within 24 to 48 hours and check the status of your application.

Please note, the average application can go up to 300 hence it is difficult even for the HR to connect with all those who have applied for the job. By you calling the HR, it makes it easier for them to understand your profile & increase your chances of getting shortlisted.

A final note on using the job portals, please ensure your resume is updated on the portal and also all details are filled, ensure you verify your email id and telephone number as portals do mention to the HR if the details are verified or not.

Be as active as you can on the job sites and search for relevant jobs only. The portals will show you results for the job you search; it is an optimized search engine tool hence don't go job shopping on these sites, be clear about what you want & search accordingly.

Also, put a professional picture of yours & give the link for your Linkedin page. It's a good idea if you have a web page for yourself. Nowadays video profiles are also accepted on portals. If you are a confident person on camera, you can create a small 2 minutes video about the skill sets you want to highlight about yourself. It is not mandatory but it does add a winning impression about your profile.

Now, before moving to the next chapter, please log in to the job portals & apply the learning from this session. You can always refer to the steps as you start updating the profile. You can also avail of the paid services offered by Portals if you think you don't have time to do this yourself due to any reason.

I conduct an exclusive session for helping job seekers to get their profile added on job portals. You can connect with me anytime for the same.

CHAPTER *Four*

Why Social Media Presence Matters and How to Use it for Job Search

I personally consider Linkedin as one of the greatest Invention to date. Linkedin made it so much easier to connect with brilliant minds across the globe so easy. It is living up to the vision of connecting talents across the Globe. There are so many success stories Linkedin created and made a huge impact on people's lives. Here are a few things that you should do to ensure you get the maximum benefit from the site.

Always keep the LinkedIn profile updated with any changes happening in your career. Nowadays HR's use LinkedIn as much as they use the portals for candidate search.

Use appropriate keywords in your profile to ensure your profile shows up when HR professionals search for a particular skill set.

Connect with Senior Professionals and HR personnel from your Industry & write a thank you note once they accept your invite, but don't start by sending your profile in the first message. You will come across as too desperate for a job change.

Secret 3: How the job search actually works.

Please note that job portals offer the Corporates/ Consultants an option to post their openings on Linked in as well along with the main posting on Portals & hence when you search jobs by clicking on the job section, you will be directed to the portal.

Let me explain, In the search bar on LinkedIn, you put the keyword as Fundamental Research/ Software developer, the drop-down next to the search bar shows various options, like, Jobs, People, Content, companies, schools, Groups. In this case, choose content & not jobs.

Now the reason for the same is, LinkedIn is a costly service for job posting & many people prefer to post it on their wall as that is a free service. When you do search content, you will see all posts including articles, posts, jobs & anything related to the keyword. Yes, it will be a little hard work but the results are great. The more connections you have, the more posts you see.

Another advantage LinkedIn offers is, when you click like or comment, people in your network will be able the see the post. Hence it is advisable whenever you see a genuine job posting, please like or share it on your page.

How to find out genuine job openings on Linkedin?

As LinkedIn is a free platform, people can post freely & many times job posting is misleading or simply put to gain more visibility on LinkedIn. A few examples are mentioned below.

A genuine job posting will have details about the role, location, official email address & optionally contact number. As long as there is an official email address, you must share your detailed resume with the recruiter.

Fake postings will simply mention, please hit like or comment & we will connect with you. Such posts are simply using you to increase their visibility on Linkedin.

Another fake post will ask you to share your resume and they will connect with you for relevant openings, please don't share your details. If you want to experiment, share your resume by deleting your phone number and email address & see if they reply to you. Chances are zero.

A lot of times, we post on our wall that we are looking for jobs and later get disappointed. No HR is looking at posts like that, posts like this will lead to nothing. Many of my female students have shared their experience with me on how boys try to connect with them online and either flirt or casual talks. There are many instances that get highlighted on LinkedIn on a regular basis.

Please use LinkedIn for professional purposes only. It is a brilliant tool for getting your dream job & to get mentors from the Industry. I would like to share a real experience that happened to one of my students, to help you understand the importance of Groups on LinkedIn.

He was an engineer, just out of college, looking for a job, he was intelligent & was seeking a good opportunity. After we set up his linked in account, he got in one of the groups of his interest. There were many professionals from the Industry in the group. There were many active discussions. He participated & posted a question to a senior in the group. That led to an active discussion between them & eventually led to a phone discussion & he referred this fresher to one of his friends in the Industry.

For a fresher coming from a small town, it was a dream come true. There are various stories that have helped people to get connected to the right people.

I have connected over 15,000 people so far on LinkedIn & I have many students that I have connected through LinkedIn whom I have helped in their job search.

Stay active on groups that you join and indulge in knowledge sharing. Today job opportunity can happen any time, Be Ready, Get Hired.

CHAPTER *Five*

The Interview Mapping Process: Questions are the New Answers

While consulting many companies, an HR head at a financial Institution, shared his experience and how frustrated he would get when he saw candidates completely unprepared for the job they were seeking desperately.

They would be blank of many questions which he asked and most of the questions he asked were from the answers they gave. For eg. The candidate would say my strength is I have a keen eye to detail. He would ask to give 2 examples of the same and they would go blank. The gap between Industry and Education was huge and that is one of the biggest challenges for decades now.

During our discussion, I came up with the questioning technique that I developed for candidates to help them anticipate questions properly.

The concept got colors when I learned the concept of Mind Maps online. An amazing tool designed by Tony Buzan led me to attend a workshop that happened in Mumbai to learn Mind Maps and combining the Questions and mapping gave birth to the Interview mapping process.

So, how does the Interview mapping process really work?

Here is a task for you. Think what comes to your mind, the moment I say think of Mango.

I believe you can imagine the color, shape, taste and different experiences around the same. For.eg. summer or maybe the king of fruit.

Now for the second word... Ready.

Rabbit. What comes to your mind? Write it here.

Now for the third word.........

PACHYDERM

If you are like most of us..... your mind has gone blank. no images. No color

This is how our brain functions.

Probably the last time you ate the Mango or seen a rabbit would be beyond 6 months yet the brain gives you all the information that you seek at the snap of the finger. The same way if you don't feed your mind on what pachyderm is, the next time you hear the word Pachyderm the mind will still be stuck. The difference between a confident candidate and a dull candidate is the preparation of the Interview mapping process.

The reason we name this as the Mapping process because similar to mind mapping you can draw various branches for every word you say which can come back to you as a question. Let's see the image of an actual mind map.

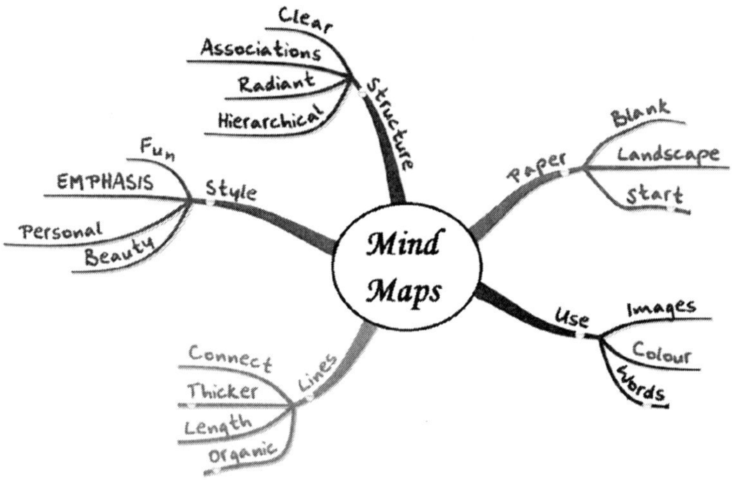

Image courtesy: *lifehack.org*

Now let's take an example of the Interview mapping process.

The candidate says, my hobbies include playing basketball and I have played at the state level for many years during college. Now if you are an interviewer what is the most common question that you would ask the candidate?

Yes, why did you not pursue basketball as a career option or what does the game teach you? Now the interviewer is clueless about anything you would say as an answer but from the answers, he/ she will pick up keywords and ask you questions around that.

Hence it is important to understand what kind of questions you want to be asked in the interview and basis that you should prepare your answer that leads to someone asking you those questions. When we do our next chapter, we want you to focus on building all the answers using the interview mapping process. This will help you anticipate the questions that can be asked and your brain is already programmed with the thoughts.

Let's see if you can do it. What and how many questions will you ask the candidate on the below statement?

I have done my Mechanical engineering then MBA finance after working for 2 years in an Automobile company. Now I am doing a Certification in business Analysis to get the role of a Business Analyst in the Finance Industry.

If you are able to build 4 questions and above you have understood the mapping process well.

Quick Recap

Interview Mapping Process

The Interview mapping process is the most effective way to Prepare for the interview, few of the benefits of using IMP is to give a direction to the interview, build confidence & do a quick analysis of how to handle questions in the Interview Room

Take a Blank card paper and start by writing your name in the center

Draw different branches from your name and every branch write a keyword. From that keyword derive more keywords. Keep doing it till you cannot think of any more keywords. Now on a separate sheet start writing questions based on the keywords you mentioned. Write as many questions as you can on every answer. Think of the shortest answers on every question. Start writing questions on the answers you have written

The best practice is to show someone the keywords and ask them to ask you questions

Eg: let's say your hobby is reading so the possible questions are

- What are you reading right now?
- Which is the last book you read?
- What did you learn from that book?
- Any specific author you follow? Why?
- What is your interest in reading?
- Why reading as a hobby

Basis the answer you give, another series of questions pop up from every keyword. So start building as many questions as you can & to build questions you will need to build answers at every level as well.

In our next chapter, we are going to focus on building the answers at every level. Let's get going.

CHAPTER *Six*

Framing the Right Image through the Answers: Understand the Context and Consequences

Interview discussions are the best part of the entire selection process. This is where the maximum time and energy is spent. The hiring decision is based on energy during the entire discussion.

Interview discussions give an opportunity to use the power of body language and words. It's an opportunity to display that you are the best fit for the role verbally as well as non-verbally.

The best interviews are a combination of stories with an example from real life to enhance the value of an answer. When kept as a 2-way interaction where you engage and ask interview questions about the company and their growth journey it shows your interest in the company and the position and enables you to gather the right information to make an intelligent decision afterward.

The questions you have prepared can be asked to different people you see. There are 2 Personal rounds, Functional/ Technical & HR Round. For the functional round, be clear and crisp around the topic.

For the HR Round, there is no right or wrong answers for any question. Every question has a context and every answer has a consequence.

The HR sub-parameters are further divided in three competencies

1. Fitment for the role, for eg, why should we hire you?
2. Stability: Eg: Where do you see yourself 5 years from now
3. Flexibility: Are you ok to relocate.

Remember, the objective of the interview is to obtain an offer. You must project yourself as the person keen to work for the company and most suitable for the role fitting in most of the parameters. During the interview, you must gather enough information concerning the position to make a decision of joining.

While discussing every question, there is a note section made for you to immediately respond the question once you understand the way to answer the question

Let's look at every question and how the favorable response should be

Tell me about yourself.

The first and the most commonly asked question in Interview is asked with the objective to check your fitment for the role. Most of the hiring decision is made the moment you start answering the question

Experienced ones: The best way to deal is to start with your name, education and current role that you are doing and major responsibilities around your work & why are you looking for the job you have applied for.

Fresher's: Start with your name, current education, any project that you want to talk and explain why you applied for this job.

In both cases, it's a good idea to start by thanking the Interviewer for the opportunity & to maintain the smile throughout the Interview.

Practice this question the most before any Interview as this question plays a very important role. Keep it simple, keep it brief and relevant.

Now, write a small introduction about yourself. It's ok to be wrong you can always correct it later. Go ahead, tell me something about yourself

Notes:

____

____

____

____

____

Now look at the Answer and check if it's relevant to the job profile. Do the mind mapping on the questions. Start by asking as many questions as you can and see if the discussion is in line with the job profile or getting diverted.

If it's getting diverted, eliminate the words that are leading to a different discussion and rewrite the Introduction.

Now for the next common question: What are your strengths?

This question can give you an advantage if you have read the Job description. There are various skill sets required for the role. Do mention a couple of strengths that you can also share a real-life example of. For eg: I was always known as the most proactive person in my class or I believe my strength lies in my dedication towards the task.

Be ready to share a few more examples of the strength mentioned. It is ok to mention just 1 or 2 strength with a good example.

Avoid *the simple generalization "I like people". It is not a good answer.*

Now time to write the answer So What is your strength?

Notes:

____

____

____

____

____

What is your weakness?

This innocent looking question can prove fatal if not handled correctly. HR's want to make sure they are not hiring anyone who will be troublesome once they come on board. They want to eliminate all the negatives and toxic people and ensure only the optimistic and positive ones get hired.

It's not the weakness the Interviewer is worried as much as they would like to know what you do about it. The interviewer probably wants reassurance that hiring you won't be a mistake.

There are 3 ways to deal with weakness, showcase your strength as your weakness, or something that you have overcome or something which is very obvious.

E.g. I consider that I get restless when I am unable to complete a task by the deadline. I have started working on planning the task in a way where I can set smaller milestones and ensure tasks are done on time.

Make sure you should use weakness that is harmless and what are you doing about it or what have you done about it

So, what is your weakness?

Notes:

____

____

____

____

____

Why should we hire you?

This is the easiest question to deal with. The answer to this question lies in the job description shared with you. Look at the qualities mentioned in the JD, look at framing the answers where you are able to justify you applying for the job.

Showcase your functional/ technical competencies along with your interpersonal skills to ensure you are a team player and also possess the right skillsets. That's what every organization looks for.

So, why should we hire you?

Notes:

____

____

____

____

____

Why do you want to work for our firm?

Never go unprepared for this question, check the website, check the company's social media presence and do good research about the company. If you know someone there ask what they feel about the organization positively. Then frame your answers to explain what is excites you about joining the company. Speak as if you already are working with this company.

Growing and learning opportunities can be an area to discuss here. Your enthusiasm matters a lot for this question. Be enthusiastic about you wanting to work there. Talk about their presence across the country, mention how you see yourself growing with the firm.

Freshers: This will be your first job, let that excitement show up that you are looking to grow with one of the best organizations in the industry and what are you expecting once you join.

Experienced: Showcasing that you are looking for challenges to solve can be a good way to lead the discussion ahead.

So, let's frame the answer: Why do you want to join us?

Notes:

____

____

____

____

____

Where do you hope to be in five years?

This question can give you an edge to get a green signal if you hit the chords right. Every organization looks for people who will stay for a long time, a lot of people answer the question by saying I want to become a Manager or I want to lead a team/ I want to be better in the Organization. Now, Let me share a concept with you to help you understand the way to handle these questions

Do you know the world's fastest-growing plant bamboo plant can grow up to 90 feet in just 6 weeks? I am sure you know but the actual fact is, it takes 5 years to come out of the ground. For 5 years, the bamboo plant grows its roots and makes it so strong so that when it comes out it becomes the world's fastest-growing plant.

One of the simplest answers to this question is Growth. Showcase that you are looking to become a subject matter expertise in the next 5 years. Don't talk about the designation, financials anything. Simply keep it about the learning opportunities. Companies want to check your stability and your interest to work with them. Showcase a learning attitude with clear growth plans. No one likes people with the unclear objective in life

So, where do you see yourself in the next t years?

Notes:

____

____

____

____

____

____

____

What interests you most about this position?

The answer should be focused on the challenge or the opportunity it provides. For e.g. Marketing helps you connect with a lot of professionals across the industry and that can help you gain a lot of insights that you can apply back to your role.

Every position has something to offer to grow and add value to the organization. Focus on what is the core area that you want to excel and how this position can help you grow within the organization

So why do you want to work in this role?

Notes:

____

____

____

____

____

____

How long do you plan to be with this company?

This question is in sync with the question of where do you see yourself in 5 years. Plan a good career path for yourself. Only 5% and fewer people have a clear career path, see where you want to reach within the organization & plan your journey accordingly.

So how long do you plan to be with the company

Notes:

____

____

____

____

____

____

What are your long- and short-term career goals?

As I mentioned only about 5% of people are clear about the career path, in one of my articles I shared a few years back I had used the example of Eagle and Snake. The eagle has a long vision, it can see its prey from far while the snake is short-sighted. The Snake serves as a food for eagle to survive but it's not vice versa. Hence when we look at our career goals, it has to be in a way where our short-term goal should add value to our long-term goal.

So, if you want to open your own restaurant in the next 10 years, working as an Operations executive in a bank won't help you build your goal. In fact, it will demotivate you and kill your eagle as well.

This is also the reason why many people compromise their long-term goals because they never planned their short term and long-term goals.

Long term can be over a decade or so where you look to be in middle management or senior management position.

E.g. *Short term:* "I want to become a subject matter expertise and the best in my current position and would seek additional responsibilities."

Long term is to upgrade my management skills and to be able to manage and lead the team for becoming one of the best places to work for the organization.

What is your short term and long-term Goal?

Notes:

____

____

____

____

____

____

Why did you leave your previous employer?

NEVER speak poorly about a former employer. You are seeking an opportunity to grow because of various or maybe one reason, be pleasant, be positive, and be honest.

If you badmouth the current employer or your boss, the impression about you will be negative as they would believe that you will do the same for their firm as well.

Your answer should be on the lines that you are seeking to work with a progressive company that offers more growth opportunities and recognition.

Notes:

Now that we have discussed the first 5 to 10 minutes of the interview discussion, I am sure you must have got a clear idea on how the start will be and how to have a strong command over the interview.

What we want you to do is start building answers for the rest of the questions below and then check if you have done it in lines with the one, we had discussed on to how the answers should be.

Do answer all the questions genuinely as this will build your confidence plus it will help your brain remember the keywords in your mind which will come handy to you.

Why are you looking for another job?

Notes:

Are you applying for other jobs?

Notes:

What are your greatest accomplishments?

Notes:

Questions for You to Ask

Your interviews should be a two-way conversation. You must ask questions and take an active role in the interview. This demonstrates the importance you place on your work and career. Asking questions gives you a chance to demonstrate your depth of knowledge in the field as well as to establish an easy flow of conversation and relaxed atmosphere between you and the interviewer. Building this kind of rapport is always a plus in an interview.

Remember, you are not just there for the interviewer to determine if you are a right for the role, you should also check if this is what you are looking for

But don't cross-examine the employer.

Ask questions requiring an explanation. Questions that can be answered with a "yes" or "no" are conversation stoppers.

Don't interrupt when the employer is answering YOUR questions.

Ask job-relevant questions. Focus on the job, the company, products, services, people.

Prior to the interview, write your list of Interest Questions and take them with you.

Ask about your potential peers, subordinates, and superiors. Take notes.

Ask the employer how he/she got where they are today.

Here are some other job interview questions you might want to rehearse & build your answers around the tips shared below

- What new skills or capabilities have you developed recently?
    - Think and answer carefully on the skillsets you have developed. Be ready to be cross-questioned on the answers you give especially if it's a functional or technical topic.
    - Be prepared thoroughly on the topic you would want to discuss.
    - Give me an example from a previous job where you've shown initiative

    - Talk about one of the things you did differently. It doesn't have to be something really great. You can talk about it even if it's a small one but you need to be confident about it.

- What have been your greatest accomplishments recently?
    - Talk about one of the achievements of your previous work. You can share the credit with team members. This showcases that you are a perfect team player and will give people the proper credit for the task they do.
- What motivates you in your work?
    - Constant problem-solving challenges and qualities related to your job role should be the answer. If you are in marketing, saying that I love to be left alone when working can leave a negative impact.
    - Look at what your job demands and position your answer accordingly.
- What qualities do you find important in a coworker?
    - Talk a few positive qualities that you look for and also mention these are also the same qualities teams can expect from you.
- What do you expect from this job?
    - Mention learning and growing opportunities from the current job and the company.

- What have you learned from your past jobs?
    - Mention a few areas that helped you learn a lot. You can also talk about how the professionalism that you have developed has come from your previous jobs.
- What were your biggest responsibilities?
    - Mention one or two responsibilities that you can talk at length if provoked more on that particular responsibilities.
- How does your previous experience relate to this position?
    - Relate a few things that you have achieved and mention how you handled or how you were able to solve or do a task and relate it to the current role.
    - The interviewer is checking your confidence level in having ownership of your role.
- What did you like most/least about your last job?
    - Mention a few things positive about your last job. Don't badmouth or say anything negative but don't go about praising too much as well. There should be a reason apart from the financial hike that you should be able to explain the job switch.
- Do you plan to study further?

- Showcase that you are a learner and would be taking certifications or courses that help you get better in your current role. A typical example of the same is as below.
- Right now I am seeking an opportunity that will help me apply the skills I possess, as I continue to progress within the organization and as per my job demands I would be looking for getting into certifications or weekend courses to help me upgrade my skills.

Now let's analyze all the answers that you wrote. Are they positive? Are they focused on the job role?

For every question that you have written, do this analysis.

Is the answer optimistic? Is it relevant to the job or role you are applying for? Is it leading to a positive discussion and will it encourage leading questions around it? Don't mention things that will divert the discussion elsewhere. For e.g, a lot of times candidates end up saying I want to be an entrepreneur in the next 5 years.

There is no harm in mentioning this as long as you are clear about what you want to do and able to relate how the current job will help you fulfill your goal. This will showcase you are someone who's focused, planner and has clear goals. This is the quality the interviewer would look for.

If the above doesn't match you, don't mention that you want to be an entrepreneur. Keep practicing all the answers. Right now focus on only the answers, once you understand the power of the body language and tone you can club both and practice.

Now let's look at one single important question that if not handled well, can destroy all the efforts that you have taken to reach the final round. In our next chapter, we will look at the Salary Negotiation.

CHAPTER Seven

Don't Just Bargain, Negotiate Your Salary Like a Pro

This is one area I have personally believed a lot of people are misguided. Even the professionals with many years of experience goof up while negotiating the salary. As per a survey by HBR, around 60% of people don't negotiate the salary, Salary hike plays a crucial role while switching jobs & because candidates are not skilled enough to negotiate their salary, they end up compromising and taking the job or simply refuse the offer.

Before accepting the salary, offer do calculate how much you would expect so that you are ok to work with a relaxed mind. Accepting something with a hope that within 6 months you will prove yourself and demand more or someone saying join now and we will evaluate your performance in 6 months and accordingly give you the hike is not acceptable & can be rejected straight away as you are up to get exploited.

No one does that. The salary is your value. The value you get depends on your overall interview and the skillsets you demonstrated. Do you ever buy a car saying I will check the performance and then give you the appropriate price?

Simply put, the dealer shows you the features and only when you are convinced that this is worth the price, you buy the car. Job selection is the same thing. Salary is the price negotiated for the value you bring to the table. Hence a complete chapter dedicated for the same. There are a few things you should know before Negotiating the Price.

Salary Negotiation is not a bargain round.

When HR asks this question, they want to check if you are greedy and if you are within the bracket of their hiring. It is also not a platform where you keep bargaining over the price, it will spoil the whole discussion and the efforts you have put in.

Salary Negotiation happens upon selection only.

Another thing to keep in mind is that Salary Negotiation happens when you are shortlisted and the actual discussion will happen in the second or third round. So be patient till you are selected and in discuss the salary when the HR comes up with the offer.

You will never know how much the organizations upper bracket of salary is

Hence it is advisable to not quote an amount first, let the HR be the first to offer the amount and from there you can take the discussion ahead.

Negotiate the value, not the price.

Never negotiate on the price hike, showcase the benefits you bring on the table and explain them again why you are the best person for the role. This will help you gain maximum benefit from the discussion.

Now, every experience level will demand a different strategy & a different approach towards the salary discussion.

Let's look at the entry-level salary negotiation process:

So, when asked this golden question of what's your salary expectation, anyone is bound to get a little nervous, especially freshers.

Step 1: Smile.

Smiling removes nervousness. Don't panic & worry, the HR is wanting to know how much would you expect as Salary & most of the time, they have fix brackets that they offer freshers. If they ask you what is your Salary expectation in the second round you have a high chance of getting this job.

As most of the time, salaries are pre-decided at the entry-level hence the scope of negotiations is very minimal & hence it is a good idea to keep the discussion simple and let them decide how much they offer for this position.

Mention that you are a fresher and you are here to be long term and grow with the organization hence salary as per the company norms for this role is ok for you.

If they insist you give a figure, politely tell them you don't have any salary figure in mind as a fresher and continue to smile. That's all. Most conversations will get over here and if you are selected, they will decide the package they want for you. You still have an advantage as you really don't know how much was the bracket, they had for this role but rest assured you will be paid fairly.

At the start of your career, focus on what the role is all about and what opportunities you have over the next 2 3 years. It's all about building the base at the start of your career.

What is the role offered to you and what you will learn from the role is more important? It's all about finding the area that you want to grow. Constantly look and evaluate the work you are doing and how that will help you.

If you want to buy a plane one day, seek a job that keeps you near the plane all the time. The more you focus on salary at the start of your career, the lesser you will earn over a period of time.

Salary Negotiation for the experienced ones:

Again, this can be really tricky as most of them expect a 30 – 40 percent hike and believe that they will get at least 20% after saying 30 but that's not the truth. Showcase the value that you add to the role without sounding too arrogant and greedy. Refer to the notes at the start of the chapter & start negotiating on the value you bring to the table.

Sorry, Mr. Shah, I haven't really thought about the salary as of now, right now the priority is to seek an opportunity that allows me to grow and also to apply my skills to the current role

I am seeking a long-term opportunity where it is a mutually beneficially situation and a win-win for us.

I haven't really thought much about the Salary as I wanted to focus on building expertise in the domain, I am getting in. I am sure, if you find me the right candidate, you will be fair.

Your answers need to be around becoming an expert over the next 3 – 4 years showcasing that you are not looking to switch your job for a long time once you get selected.

The Salary Negotiation for 10 years plus

This is where you have an edge of showcasing how you have made a difference in the previous organizations and how you can ensure value add happens here. Focus on being a subject matter expertise in your domain and negotiate accordingly.

In all the three cases, please ensure you are not the one asking for the raise. Let the HR be the first one to come up with an offer.

Few example statements for your reference are

1. I really don't know how much you would offer to a person like me for this role
2. I believe you are a better judge for this question, based on our discussion I will leave the decision on to you for the Salary part.

3. I am seeking a long-term growth opportunity, I am sure if you find me a suitable candidate, you will be fair to me.

Please note the HR will also negotiate and use sentences to get you at a lower package, stick to 2 things one that you bring value to the table & second you are seeking a long-term association.

You need to be very confident while Negotiating your salary & we highly recommend practice the Salary negotiation 10 times more as compared to other questions.

If you fail to practice & goof up on your answers, chances of not getting the job become higher. We sincerely recommend a lot of practice on this question. This is also the reason to make this as a separate chapter.

CHAPTER *Eight*

Telephone & Video Interview

In this section, we will jump straight to the learning on the dos and don'ts for the Telephone & Video Interview.

Telephone and Video Interviews are common norms in the Industry & the biggest advantage is the time saved for both, the candidate as well the Interviewer. Let's look at them one by one. The Telephone Interview has been there for a long time & there are various articles and blogs written about how to be prepared for this Interview.

The first thing we recommend is to download true caller app on your phone, this helps you identify the caller. There are 2 reasons for this, first is we are so accustomed to saying hello casually on the phone we would end up saying something casually.

Second, if you are in a crowded place & pick up the phone, it can lead to disturbance and disturb the conversation. Whenever we start the conversation with strangers the initial few seconds are a little awkward.

Now imagine if you know who's calling you, in this case, you will be better prepared to answer the call. Your tone will be confident from the start of the conversation. You are mentally into the conversation from the beginning.

On Interview calls, you can start by saying your name will make you stand out against the other candidates who start by Hello, then Yes this is Amit Kumar speaking and so on. What we have done is identified the major 5 steps that can help you prepare you well for any Telephonic Interview.

Listening

The most important part of the telephonic part is your ability to listen well. This means patiently hearing the questions, acknowledging the important questions and taking a pause to ensure you don't talk over the Interviewer. This ensures you have understood the question well & also leaves a good impression even before you answer the actual question.

You should also acknowledge when the Interviewer is taking for some time, an occasional hmm and ok is a good option.

Taking Notes

To ensure you are not under pressure, you should make notes on the questions and also on the answers you are giving to the Interviewer. This helps you recall the conversation faster and also as a clue for a few answers as the discussion progresses.

For eg. As mentioned earlier, I believe that..... That as mentioned earlier becomes easy when you made the notes properly.

Keep your resume handy

Nothing is as good as keeping the resume handy while the telephone Interview is on. If you are sitting on your laptop, just make sure only the resume is open, if you keep the mailbox or any social site open, it will distract you.

Face the wall

The idea behind this is to avoid any distractions and ensuring you are not disturbed by others.

Ask Questions

Technology has made Interviews easier through the telephone and Video. Yet it comes with its disadvantages as there is an absence of physical presence and face to face vs over the technology tool is completely different

Let's start with the Telephonic round preparation first

In the telephonic round, you cannot see the interviewer and cannot see the reaction on the other side of the line. So, you have to assume that he is sitting in front of you and conversing. Here are some tips that you should always keep in mind.

Listen carefully: The absence of the person present in front of you can lead you to have many thoughts running in mind and hence it might happen that you are unable to listen to the Interviewer. It is always a possibility to miss out and misunderstand words on the telephone.

This can lead to miscommunication and you may not be able to understand the question correctly and perhaps give unsatisfactory answers. Also, it might make the interviewer think that you are not interested in the interview. So, be calm and pay attention to the Interviewer. It's a good idea to face a blank wall while talking on the phone, it increases your confidence level.

Take the call in a quiet and peaceful place. Too much noise can distract you and you may lose your focus. And, even the interviewer may find it difficult to communicate clearly, leading to confusion and agitation for both parties.

Do not pause for too long or add too many fillers: Pausing for too long or adding fillers like 'hmmm', 'ahh' etc make the interviewer doubt your knowledge and confidence. The interviewer cannot see you and as such, long pauses can actually create confusion and can be disturbing during the conversation. So, never pause for too long or use too many fillers. If you need time to think about something, state it upfront.

Avoid distractions: This is one area that can prove fatal during interviews.

Today there are constant notification pop-ups on the mobile and most of them are highly distractive. Also, with so many technology devices around us, it has become really difficult to stay focused. The first thing to do is keep the notifications off while taking a call, especially when you use headphones for the call. Keep all other devices switched off and face the wall while taking the call.

If you are in office premises, inform the interviewer that you are getting in a closed chamber and ask them the hold, they will appreciate your gesture. Keep only the things handy that you need during the interview. Pen paper and a copy of your resume should be enough.

Be prepared

Be prepared all the time. Even if you are home, dress in formals and take the call as if you are meeting the person face to face. Formal dressing adds to your confidence and also ensures your body language and tone is in sync for the discussion, Formal dressing sets the mood and gets you in a mental state to discuss professionally.

Ensure the phone battery is charged and the network is good for the call. If you are facing connectivity issues, request if you can call back and discuss or ask the person to hold as you move to a better network.

Inform your family members not to disturb you during the Interview if you are taking the call from home. Ensure there are no background disturbances like music, television sound. The room temperature should be in control. Too hot or too cold will cause irritation and affect the tone and body language during the interview.

Remove the call waiting option from your phone the last thing you probably need is someone calling you constantly in the background when you are trying to focus on the call.

Know your subject area well. Be clear about your career goals and how you plan to connect the same to the job you are applying for. Practice the Mapping process discussed in the previous chapter. Make as many questions as you can on the answers given and ensure you are focusing on giving answers only to ensure you are asked what you want to be asked.

Make notes during the call. This can come handy to connect the dots while discussing and you can always refer to these important pointers during the follow-up call.

Stay Calm and Cool

Interviews can be nerve breaking and frustrating especially the functional/ technical round. Remember, the selection is not in your control, only the efforts are. The best you can do is have a conversation and showcase your skills.

It is very obvious that if you don't know the answer to a particular question, nervousness can sulk in. Don't start searching for the answer immediately online just because you cannot be seen on the phone. Our body language and tone are impacted and the person on the other side can figure that without even seeing you.

Stay calm, stay composed, if you don't know the answer, let the other person know you don't know the answer as of now but if given a chance will learn the same. This will also put a good impression on the interviewer that you are someone who will learn things as per the job demand and not hide or give excuses when it comes to work deliveries.

Few more things to keep in mind while giving telephone Interview:

Have smaller sips of water during the conversation, Phone interviews can take a lot of time based on the job profile and your experience and the interest that has been developed, ensure you are hydrated enough that you sound confidence and non-chirpy.

A smile can be heard on the phone: Just like formal dressing boosts your confidence, a smile can work wonders. When we smile, our brain releases a chemical called endorphins and these endorphins are responsible for making us feel happy, and they also help lower stress levels. This is one of the biggest stress busters during the Interview discussion. Start making a habit from now on to constantly smile every time you speak to anyone on the phone until it becomes a habit.

Video Interviews:

Over the last few years, there has been an increase in video interviews over Skype, hangout/ Duo and this given edge to the pot of potential hiring.

The advantage of Video Interviews is the presence of body language and expressions. Over video calls, you have face for the voice that you are hearing.

Apart from applying everything the same way that you would in a telephonic interview you need to pay attention to a few more things.

Your background should be clean and tidy. For eg, if you are taking the call from home, ensure there is no stuff lying around the room. A messy room gives the impression that you are an unorganized person while a clean environment around you gives the impression that you are an organized person. If possible, sit against a clean wall facing the camera.

If in office premises, take the call in a closed chamber with you facing outside the chamber and the interviewer should be able to see the outside of the building. While discussion, we tend to look at the screen to see the person as we have become habituated with so many personal video calls.

During Interviews start looking at the camera, the interviewer is looking at the screen and when you see the camera directly, it is like you are maintaining eye contact with them. This is a sign of confidence during the conversation.

Ensure the network connection is good. Wi-fi connection is better so if you have the option, connect through wi-fi and keep all other devices switched off. If you are taking the call through your laptop, close all the other folders and files to avoid any kind of disturbance or distraction.

Another thing while Video interviews are to use the power of body language. Expressions are noticed hence show the enthusiasm to communicate through your tone, your smile and also through the proper use of hand gestures. In our session on body language, we will understand the power of body language in detail.

CHAPTER *Nine*

The Group Discussion

Group Discussion (GD's) are mistaken to be an elimination round, as these are conducted when there are many walk-ins or in Campus placement. It is a partial truth; GD's helps the Interviewer understand the personality of the candidates and accordingly offer them roles in the Organization.

Irrespective of all the different views about GD, it is still an important part of the selection process and also a little tough as you have to ensure you are selected over others for the Personal discussion round.

The Pre- Preparation for GD for Freshers:

Read beyond just your academics, GD topics are generally around current affairs and any sensitive topics that are in the news recently. It could be around politics, economy, society or general topics. Keep yourself updated on the latest happening around you.

Research on the news and don't let the only side of the news make an opinion about something, this can lead you to have strong views about something and make you argumentative when some gets in discussion with a different viewpoint

Please note, there are really no correct side in the GD round, everyone is just stating their knowledge and views on the particular topic.

Get in a practice of appreciating other people's views and knowledge.

Getting in the Group Discussion

Once the Interviewer announces a particular topic, they are going to evaluate everyone on few parameters as below

1. Speaking Skills
2. Listening Skills
3. Overall Attitude
4. Team Player
5. Leadership & Ownership
6. Knowledge on the topic

Once the GD begins, look around and most of the time there will be someone wanting to jump into the topic and immediately start talking and many times, many will start talking at the same time. This is a great opportunity for you to control the environment and give the GD a direction as a leader. You can suggest how the time can be utilized and everyone get a chance to speak, so divide the time into 2 rounds so that everyone speaks two times.

Then offer the opportunity to someone to start first and then they can go clockwise or anticlockwise or just raise the hand and speak.

You can think of strategies of how you want to get this whole discussion done. There is no right or wrong way, as long as people are engaged and you are either leading or supporting the leader to ensure the GD is completed.

Acknowledge people for presenting good ideas on the table but never take sides, remember no one is wrong or right, they are just sharing the knowledge.

Make notes and give people the credit for the knowledge they share. Make notes of people's names and address them by their name while rephrasing what they said.

Never get in correcting someone during the GD round and if someone tells you that your knowledge is incorrect, share with them the source and ask them for the source and let them know that you will be happy to correct yourself if your knowledge is incorrect

Be polite and generous during the discussion, request people to give chance to people who remain silent for a long time.

Don't interrupt and also if someone interrupts you be firm yet tell them politely to not interrupt you as they will also get their chance to present their ideas.

As a successful leader in the GD, keep control of time or if you are not the leader offer the leader that you can keep the tab of time. Time Management skills are very important for the selection, this attitude describes that you are someone who will work in the deadlines.

Your body language and tone are very important, have an open body language and pleasant tone and don't get in any verbal argument with anyone. The body language changes when we get in an argument or a disagreement, please remember you are getting evaluated, the person dragging you in the argument is making sure both of you get rejected. You don't have to win the argument; you have to win the Interviewer. Be firm yet polite that everyone has the right to their view.

Do quick recap towards the end of the GD, this is also a sign of ownership that you take.

Remember GD rounds are supposed to be discussed and not heated debates. Keep them that way.

Some Important times to remember

Things to do:

Take initiate to talk only if you know the subject well & are confident

Take notes while listening to others in case you don't know the subject well.

Back up your point with facts and figures & mention the source wherever needed.

If everyone is randomly sharing their thoughts, make smaller contribution of about 30 seconds 2 to 3 times.

Let others also share their views and knowledge.

Summarize the discussion if the group has not reached a conclusion.

Don'ts:

Don't be the first one to Initiate the discussion if you don't possess sufficient knowledge about the topic.

Don't over speak, intervene and cut people while speaking

Don't get in arguments & have harsh conversations

Don't speak off the topic about irrelevant things

Don't try to dominate others and put others in an embarrassing situation by asking them to speak. Everyone can choose their chance to speak when they are ready.

Sharing the link for an amazing GD round conducted. This will help you prepare better. This video is prepared by Wipro & Mcgraw Hill's education.

https://www.youtube.com/watch?v=E-Cq06fegI4

The task for this chapter: Sharing a few topics that you should start researching. Also, do research online to see any new additions of the topic that might come for your next discussion. Even the HR's would go online and search the topics so be smarter and look for topics that are hot and recent and start preparing accordingly.

1. The slowdown in Indian Economy in 2019: Temporary or Structural
2. Disinvestment on CPSE central public sector enterprises: Good step to augment public expenditure or selling the family silver

3. RCEP Agreement: Right step for national interest or running away from competition
4. India improves Ease of Doing Business Ranking: Real or chimera
5. Article 370 Abrogation: Correcting old folly or thrusting nationalistic agenda
6. Single-Use Plastic Ban:
7. Delhi Air Pollution: Man-made Crisis or fall out of industrialization
8. Chandrayaan 2: A failed mission or a stepping stone for future glory
9. Hong Kong Protests: Rebel against China or pro-democracy fight
10. US-China Trade Talks: A political drama or renegotiation of rules of game.

Source: mbauniverse.com

CHAPTER *Ten*

The Power of Body Language: Never Underestimate the Importance of Nonverbal's

Powerful body language can help you win any deal. Most successful sales professionals and leaders use body language to win over their clients and subordinates.

Body language is an art and once you master the skill, you can have anything that you want. Most of the Interviewers are experts in reading the person's body language. They are trained to check the candidate's body language and through body language, they can find out how genuine is the person is and is he/ she truthful about the answers. This helps them hire the right person for the job.

The personality of anyone can be read through by their expressions, hand gestures and movements, eye movements, and overall posture and gesture.

Look at the image below:

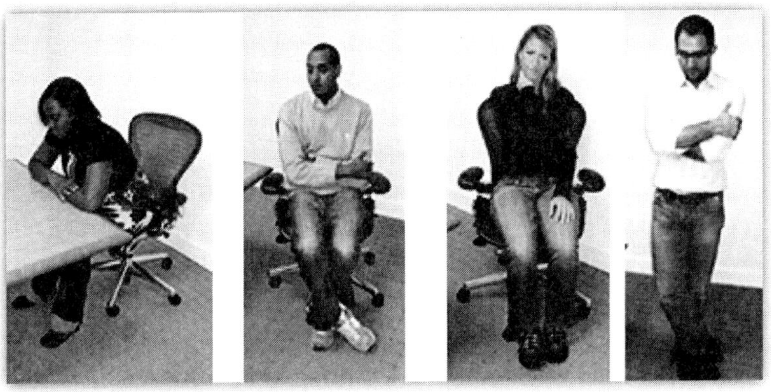

Image courtesy: *Frontiers*

Image courtesy: *telegraph.com*

We communicate 90% through nonverbal i.e through our tone and body language, hence it is very easy to make a quick analysis about anyone just by looking at their body language, including the way they sit, they stand and they walk or talk.

Our answers and body language need to be in sync all the time. The first step towards this is to practice your answers not just in words but also through our hand gesture, our expression, and the entire body. Let us start by looking at handshakes and the concept of body space. The study of body space is called Proxemics, look at the image below

When we meet someone for the first time, we are moving from a public space to social space, by doing a handshake we are invading in their personal or Intimate space and this can work against you.

A lot of times to showcase we are confident, we offer a handshake to the Interviewer, but it can backfire especially if it's offered to a lady. Unless we don't interact with the other person for some time, it is a good idea to operate from the social space.

If the Interviewer is offering the handshake, reply with a confident handshake, not too dull and not too pressurized one. A simple handshake, firm grip, 3 times movement in the air and then leaving it. Maintain body distance for 1 foot, and maintain eye contact while doing the handshake.

The second is eye contact: Maintain eye contact all the time with a pleasant smile during the entire Interview. If it's a panel Interview, maintain equal eye contact with everyone. This indicates that you are a confident person and knows your subject well.

The third is your hand movements, Studies indicate that when people speak with confidence & truth, they do a lot of hand movement and when they lie, their hands are still. Still, hand also indicates nervousness or rigid behavior.

When you speak with your hands open and up facing the sky, it indicates a very open person to talk with and nothing to hide about anything. This is a sign of most of the confident speakers today.

Tilting head little towards the left or nodding head is another gesture that can work wonders, this ensures you are actively participating in the discussion and are engaged with the Interviewer.

Our body style communicates a lot, slouching body indicates nervousness or desperate for the job. An upright posture with a firm neck and hand movements at the stomach level indicates you are prepared thoroughly for any questions. Crossed hands and crossed legs indicate hiding something or low on confidence.

Standing or sitting with arms crossed across your chest is a sign of defensive body language. It indicates you're not engaged or defensive against the other person's viewpoint. You may appear self-centered or stubborn.

The hands can be crossed when the room temperature is very cold if that's the case request the Interviewer to switch off the AC or your body language can be misread. When you tap your fingers or constantly shake your leg, you look impatient and want to leave for some reason or you are nervous about waiting. There are various ways crossing the legs is interpreted, if you cross the legs at the ankle, you are trying to hide or you are trying to control the conversation. If you cross them at the knee level, you appear confident and comfortable, but if you point your knees from the other person, it indicates that you are uncomfortable with the other person. The best way is to keep the legs firm on the ground with the one-foot distance between them.

Looking at the ground makes you look low on confidence and a weak person. The weakest body language is when you head down and hold your neck with one hand. Looking at the floor or ground makes you appear weak and unconfident. Unless there's something you need to discuss down there, you need to keep your eyes on the level of the other person's face. When you break eye contact, as you should every few seconds, try looking to the side.

Unlike in movies, where hair curling is a sign of happiness and falling in love, in the Interview room, you will be pretended like you are nervous and uncomfortable as you constantly twist your hair.

Rubbing or Touching Your Nose

Rubbing/ touching the nose in the Interview is a complete no-no. It means you are dishonest & that is the last thing you want in the Interview room. Also watch for the Interviewer's gesture, if they rub their nose about something, you better don't trust them.

When you stand with your hand behind your back, you are showing that you are an aggressive person with anger and authority issues. It can make people very uncomfortable talking to you

Standing with Your Hands on Your Hips

This can be a deceiving pose, while in some cases, it can mean that you are feeling angry and may behave aggressively & standing with hands-on hips with a big smile on your face can simply mean that you're enthusiastic and ready to get something done.

How to change your body Language:

There is a concept called Power Poses. I recommend that you must watch the video shared by Amy Cuddy on the power of body language in which she talks about power poses and how to fake it till you become it.

Search AMY Cuddy Ted talk on youtube and watch it once to understand the power you can create.

Another Video I would recommend is by a speaker Kanan Tandi in her TedX talks shares how it is so easy to read the body language signs.

So, go ahead and watch these videos and we will see you in the next chapter.

CHAPTER *Eleven*

Take Action

First thing first. Heartiest congratulations on completing all the chapters. I am happy that you have done the tasks in the chapters and practicing the exercises mentioned. If not, nothing is lost yet, I am sure you must have found the content relevant and start over again and do the exercises. The best way to be ready is to start taking actions.

Now go ahead and take action for practicing the tasks. Here are the quick key takeaways from the book one for time for you.

- First, Prepare a professional profile for yourself. You can connect with us any time for any assistance on the resume building and feedback on the resume prepared.
- Second, get active on Job portals and social media sites like Linkedin. They are amazing platforms to connect you with the right professionals across the Industry.
- Third, Do the interview mapping process correctly. Write as many questions as you can from the keywords derived.
- The more you practice this part, the higher the confidence level while facing the Interview
- Next prepare for the answers that suit you and make you the competent person for the role. Ensure to

keep the answer crisp and concise and be ready for examples for the qualities you mention.

- Negotiate the Salary and don't bargain. There is a difference between the two. Negotiate the salary based on the value you add to the role and not based on how much you were drawing last.
- Knowyourcutoffandifthesalarynegotiationdoesn't come to a win-win to both, don't compromise. Politely refuse the offer.
- Be prepared for Interview on the telephone and video anytime.
- Be professional and ensure you are using the tone effectively to create a favorable response. Be smiling always on the Call.
- The group discussion is a wonderful platform for you to showcase your leadership abilities and ownership.
- Handle Group discussion with total control over the discussion by being proactive and leading the discussion in the right direction
- Encourage participation from everyone and be optimistic about the topic.
- Don't bully or target the weak ones and don't get in or encourage any arguments or unpleasant talks. One of the guaranteed ways to get rejected in the GD round is to show some down to prove yourself

superior. GD is your platform to showcase you are a team player.

- Understand the power of your body language and make the most of it. Use gestures and expressions to your advantage.
- Take action and start searching for jobs through the right means.

Now Practice, Practice and Practice… like Amy Cuddy says in her TED Talk, fake it till you become it.

We wish you all the best and hope this book has added value to you in preparing you for your next Interview.

We look for your feedback and suggestions to make this book better. Please leave your comments on the Amazon site and share your feedback on praddeepkhanapure@gmail.com

Good luck and Be job-ready... Get hired.

Thank you for your time.